CONTENTS

Earth's Last Wild Places

White wastes

The polar regions, the Arctic and Antarctic, are the Earth's last two great wildernesses. For much of the year, they are shrouded in darkness, intensely cold and blanketed by ice and snow. In summer, they are bathed in sunlight, and the Arctic plains are carpeted with flowers.

Humans struggle to survive in these hostile conditions. Yet surprisingly, the Arctic is home to abundant wildlife, as are the seas and coasts around Antarctica. Their very remoteness makes the polar regions important for scientific study. They also have a major effect on world weather patterns, as they greatly influence the world's winds and ocean currents.

Emperor penguins live on the icy Antarctic coasts.

4

Scientists visit the Arctic and Antarctic to research the climate, wildlife and the ice itself. The study of ice sheets and of ancient ice found deep in glaciers can reveal evidence of pollution and of the Earth's past climate.

Polar regions in danger

Two centuries ago, the polar regions were almost completely untouched and unspoiled. Indeed, the Antarctic continent was only discovered in 1820. In the last 200 years, however, there has been a lot of change. Parts of the Arctic have been damaged by mining, and pollution from distant industries has been carried by winds and deposited in crystal-clear Arctic streams. The polar regions have now been threatened by a new danger: warmer weather. Although the Earth's climate has varied greatly in the past, recent rising temperatures have begun to melt polar ice which has existed for thousands of years. Human activities are responsible for the current warming, and we must act now to save these unique habitats. This book explains what makes the polar regions special, what damage we humans are causing and how we can help to save these special worlds.

CHAPTER ONE

What Are the Polar Regions?

The ends of the Earth

The polar regions are the areas surrounding the North and South Poles, the most northerly and southerly points on Earth. The Arctic is named after the northerly Great Bear constellation (in Greek, *arktos*). Antarctic means "opposite Arctic".

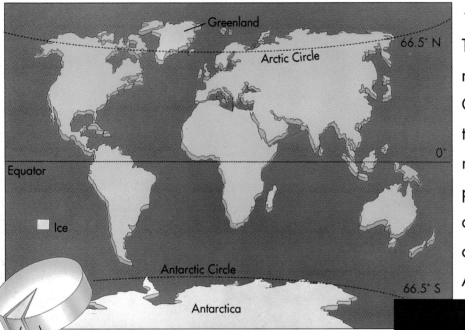

Greenland

66.5° N

Arctic Circle

0°

Equator

☐ Ice

Antarctic Circle

66.5° S

Antarctica

90% Ice-free land

10% Ice-covered land

Today, ice covers roughly 10% of the Earth's surface. Nearly all of this ice is found in the great ice sheets of Antarctica and Greenland.

◄ Polar limits

The limits of the polar regions are marked by the Arctic and Antarctic Circles. These imaginary lines circle the Earth at 66.5 degrees latitude north and south of the Equator. The polar regions are difficult to show on flat maps like this one because of the Earth's curved shape. Often, Antarctica is not shown at all.

Icy wastes

Antarctica is the world's coldest continent. Some parts of the Arctic are almost as cold. For up to six months each year, there is no Sun to warm them. When the Sun returns, it never rises far above the horizon. Much of its heat is absorbed in the atmosphere or reflected back into space by polar ice.

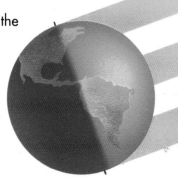

Little heat reaches the poles because the Sun's rays have more atmosphere to travel through there than at the Equator.

——— Because the Sun's rays hit the poles at an angle, they are spread over a wide area, and it never gets very warm. Animals like the Arctic fox (above) have adapted to the icy conditions.

The polar seasons

Our Earth experiences seasons because it tilts on its axis as it moves around the Sun. As one hemisphere leans towards the Sun, it has summer, while the other leans away, and has winter. The polar regions have extreme seasons, with great variation in day length. In summer, the Sun never sinks below the horizon for days on end and it is light at midnight (right). In winter, the Sun never rises.

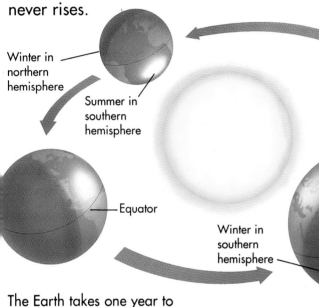

Winter in northern hemisphere

Summer in southern hemisphere

Summer in northern hemisphere

Equator

Winter in southern hemisphere

The Earth takes one year to make a full circuit of the Sun.

Cooling the world ▶

The polar regions have a cooling effect on the world's weather. Winds and ocean currents (right) carry cold polar air and water to other parts of the globe. This helps to regulate temperatures worldwide, so plants and animals can thrive.

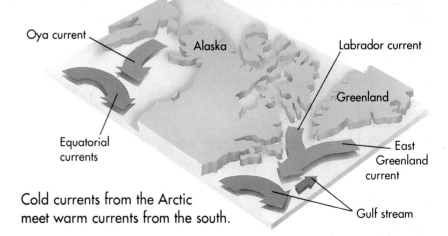

Oya current

Alaska

Labrador current

Greenland

Equatorial currents

East Greenland current

Cold currents from the Arctic meet warm currents from the south.

Gulf stream

Q: The climate (regular weather pattern) of the polar regions is cold, but how cold, exactly?

A: Air temperatures seldom rise above 10°C, even on mild days in the Arctic. In winter, they often drop to –40°C at night. Antarctica's climate is even colder. The average temperature at the South Pole is –49°C.

The Arctic

The Arctic and Antarctic are both icy places, but in other ways they are very different. The Arctic is mostly an ice-covered ocean, ringed by the continents of North America, Europe and Asia, and by Greenland, the world's largest island. The Antarctic is mainly land.

Top of the world

Most of the area inside the Arctic Circle is covered by the icy Arctic Ocean. From the North Pole in the centre, the Arctic stretches for 2,160 km to all points south.

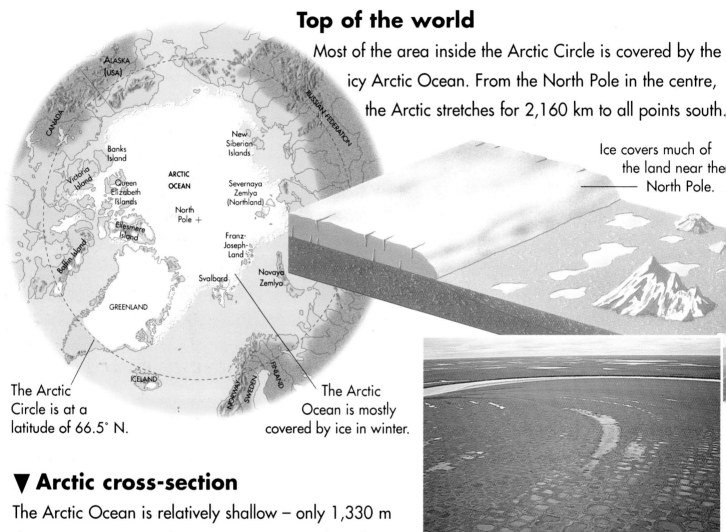

Ice covers much of the land near the North Pole.

The Arctic Circle is at a latitude of 66.5° N.

The Arctic Ocean is mostly covered by ice in winter.

▼ Arctic cross-section

The Arctic Ocean is relatively shallow – only 1,330 m deep on average. Undersea mountains rise from the sea bed. Beneath the floating ice, the water is calm, dark and very cold. In winter, a large area of ocean freezes over. In summer, sea ice only covers about half its winter extent.

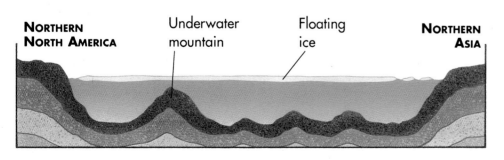

NORTHERN NORTH AMERICA

Underwater mountain

Floating ice

NORTHERN ASIA

▲ Tundra

Thick ice covers most land near the North Pole. Further south, the snow and ice melt in summer to reveal the barren, treeless lowlands of the tundra. Beneath the topsoil is a layer of permanently frozen ground, called permafrost.

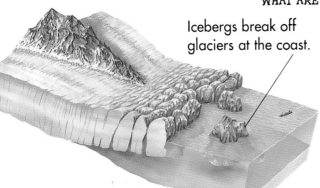

Icebergs break off glaciers at the coast.

◀ Glaciers and icebergs

Land ice in the Arctic is formed of tightly-packed snow. From high ground inland, icy glaciers slowly flow down towards the sea. At the water's edge, the ice breaks off, or 'calves', to form towering icebergs. These can be a danger to shipping if they float too far south.

◀ Eskers and pingos

In summer, the tundra is littered with lakes separated by long, narrow ridges called eskers. The melted water cannot drain through the permanently frozen ground, so it collects in pools. Mounds called pingos occur where underground ice has forced the ground up into a dome.

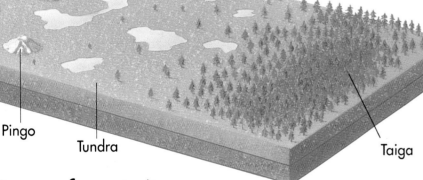

Pingo

Tundra

Taiga

▲ Warm coasts

In cold parts of the world, the seas are generally warmer than the land. This is certainly the case in the Arctic, where the ocean warms the edges of the icy landmasses. This is one reason why most Arctic towns and villages have sprung up on the coast.

Dense forests ▶

A belt of dense, evergreen forests called the taiga lies south of the tundra. Some scientists define the limits of the Arctic as the edge of this great belt of trees.

TALKING·POINT·

Q: Drifting icebergs can threaten shipping in the North Atlantic and Pacific Oceans. Have they caused any major accidents?

A: The most famous sea disaster ever was caused by an iceberg. In 1912, the luxury liner *Titanic* struck a large iceberg while crossing the Atlantic on its maiden voyage. It sank quickly, and 1,513 people died.

The Antarctic

The Antarctic is quite different from the Arctic. In contrast to the far north, most of the area inside the Antarctic Circle is occupied by land. The vast, icy continent of Antarctica is Earth's fifth largest landmass, twice the size of Australia. The continent is cut through by a high mountain range, the Transantarctic Mountains, and surrounded by the icy, stormy waters of the Southern Ocean. Scientists now believe that East and West Antarctica are separate landmasses under the ice.

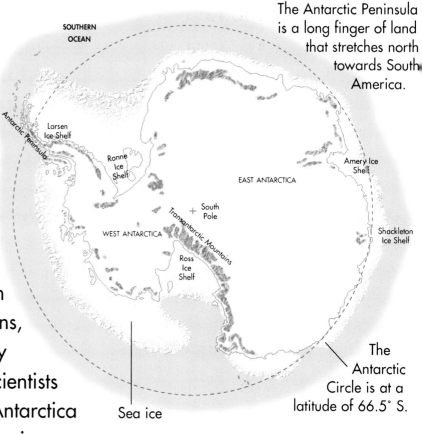

The Antarctic Peninsula is a long finger of land that stretches north towards South America.

The Antarctic Circle is at a latitude of 66.5° S.

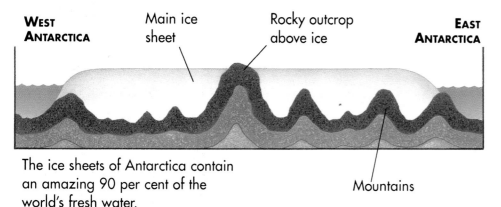

The ice sheets of Antarctica contain an amazing 90 per cent of the world's fresh water.

Profile of Antarctica

Almost all land in Antarctica is covered by a thick ice sheet, 5 km deep in places. The ice is formed of layers of packed-down snow. The tops of the highest mountains break through the ice to form rocky outcrops, but most of the land lies deep below.

Ice shelves ▶

Antarctic land ice flows slowly down towards the sea in glaciers. On the coast, ice spreads out over the sea to form huge floating shelves. The largest shelf, the Ross Ice Shelf, is the size of France. In summer, some ice breaks off the shelves to form giant, flat-topped icebergs.

Freezing and melting ▼

Seen from space, Antarctica appears to grow and shrink over the year. In autumn, the Antarctic seas start to freeze over. From coastal areas, the ice spreads northwards at a rate of 3 km a day. In winter, ice covers hundreds of kilometres of ocean, twice the area that is frozen in summer.

The distant past

Antarctica has not always been as cold as it is now. Many millions of years ago, the continent was located much closer to the Equator. This explains why fossils of ferns, ammonites, plants and animals of warmer regions, and even dinosaur fossils have been found here. Later, the section of the Earth's crust bearing Antarctica drifted very slowly south to reach its present position. Rocks and minerals found in Antarctica are also proof of its warmer past.

Fossil ammonite from Antarctica

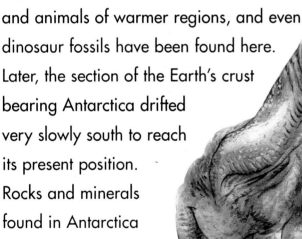

Scientists believe that the Antarctic was warmer when *Hypsilophodon* lived there, 145 million years ago.

TALKING POINT

Q: Antarctica has high mountain ranges. How high are the tallest mountains?

A: The highest peak on Antarctica is Mt Vinson, 5,139 m high. It is taller than the highest peak in the European Alps, Mont Blanc. On average, Antarctica is the world's highest continent by far – almost three times higher than any other landmass. Yet the great weight of the icecap pushes much of the land below sea level. If the icecap melted, the land would rise by several hundred metres.

CHAPTER TWO

Life in the Polar Regions

Life in the icy seas

Plant and animal plankton

Polar seas are home to an amazing variety of creatures. The great whales and giant squid are huge. Others, such as krill, are tiny, but all the larger creatures ultimately depend on them for food.

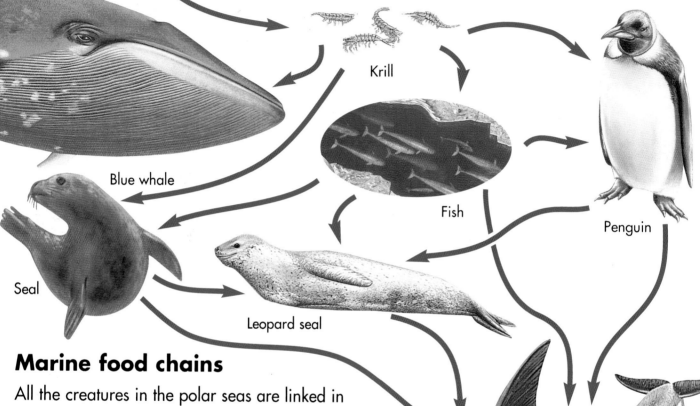

Krill

Blue whale

Fish

Penguin

Seal

Leopard seal

Marine food chains

All the creatures in the polar seas are linked in a great web of life. At the base of the food chain, tiny plant plankton are eaten by animal plankton, which in turn are consumed by krill. Krill are eaten by fish, seals, penguins and seabirds, which are hunted by top predators such as leopard seals and killer whales.

Killer whale

Antarctic marine food chain

◄ Abundant food

All life in polar waters ultimately depends on microscopic plant plankton. These tiny plants use energy from sunlight to feed and grow. In spring, when the sea ice melts, the plankton multiply at a great rate. This is known as plankton bloom. Sea creatures from warmer latitudes arrive to take advantage of the abundant food.

Expert divers

Penguins are seabirds of the southern hemisphere. Seven species live in Antarctica or on the nearby islands. Penguins cannot fly, but are superb swimmers and deep divers. They launch themselves into the sea from the edge of the floating pack ice. Underwater, they use their flipper-like wings to "fly" through the water as they chase after fish. Oily feathers help to protect them from the cold.

Predators

The leopard seal (right) is the penguins' chief predator. In the Arctic, polar bears are the fiercest predators and their favourite food is seal meat. You may be surprised to know that most scientists class polar bears as sea creatures. Although they do come on land, they spend most time swimming in the ocean or clambering about on sea ice.

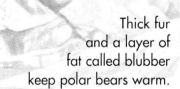

Thick fur and a layer of fat called blubber keep polar bears warm.

Q: Temperatures in polar seas are often close to freezing. How do marine animals survive?

A: Seals, whales and polar bears keep warm in icy waters with the help of a thick layer of fatty blubber. This layer, just beneath the skin, provides insulation and helps keep body heat in. Some sea mammals also have coarse fur which traps warmth. Seabirds have oily feathers that repel water.

Life on land

Arctic bilberry

Plants and animals also live on land in the Arctic. Some visit only for the summer, and spend their winters further south. Antarctica is too cold and hostile for plants and animals to live inland.

Life on Antarctica ▶

The coasts are the warmest places to live on Antarctica, thanks to the warming influence of the sea. Close to the shore, mosses, lichens and a very few flowering plants grow. They feed the only land animals in Antarctica, which are tiny spiders and insects, such as this springtail.

▼ Arctic food chain

The Arctic has many land animals. Each species is adapted to survive in this frozen world. In summer, plants flower and insects hatch out. Grasses and lichens feed herbivores (plant-eating animals), such as caribou and lemmings. In turn, these creatures feed carnivores (meat-eaters), such as wolves and snowy owls.

Arctic saxifrage plant

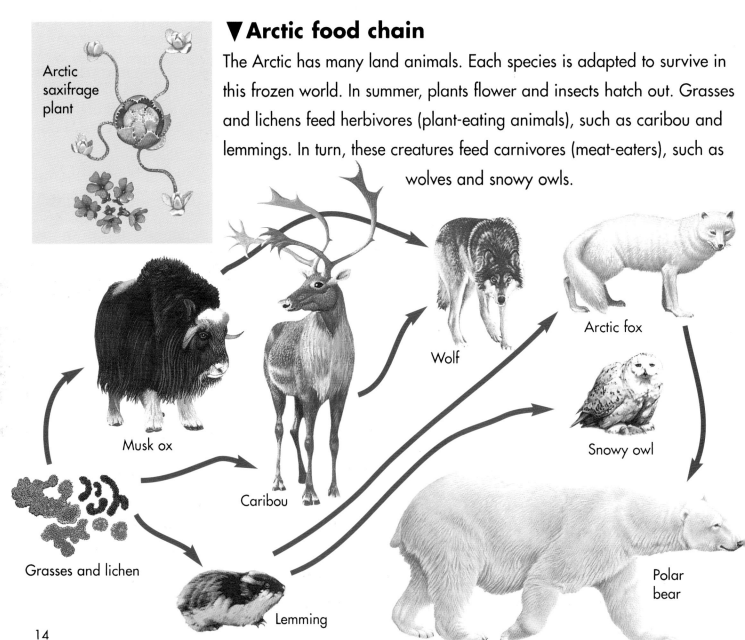

Musk ox

Caribou

Wolf

Arctic fox

Snowy owl

Grasses and lichen

Lemming

Polar bear

Hide and seek

In the Arctic, there are no trees or big plants for animals to hide behind. Instead, animals hide from enemies or prey using natural camouflage. The colours and patterns of their fur and feathers blend in with the background, making them hard to see. Some creatures, such as the Arctic fox, have fur of a different colour in summer and winter.

Arctic fox's brown summer coat matches the tundra.

Its white winter coat matches the snow.

Caribou spend winter in southern forests. In spring, they travel north to breed in the Arctic, crossing vast, barren lands and fast-flowing rivers. In autumn, the young calves return south with the herd when they are just a few months old.

Migration

A few hardy animals survive in the Arctic all year round. Many species, including caribou – reindeer – and Canada geese (right) visit only for the summer, and spend winter in the warmer south. Both mammals and birds travel a long distance in spring and autumn to reach their summer breeding and winter feeding grounds. These regular yearly journeys are called migrations.

TALKING POINT

Some land animals spend their whole life in the freezing north.

Q: How do they survive the winters?

A: Musk oxen, lemmings, Arctic foxes and birds called ptarmigan spend winter in the north. They grow an extra-thick coat of fur or feathers in autumn. Lemmings survive by burrowing into the snow, where temperatures are warmer than above ground.

Polar people

Despite the freezing, hostile conditions, people have lived in the Arctic for thousands of years. Arctic groups include the Inuit of North America, the Saami of Scandinavia and the peoples of Siberia, in Russia, shown on this map. Antarctica has never been inhabited. The first "settlers" were scientists in the 20th century, who set up bases to conduct research.

■ Inuit   □ Yakut
■ Samoyed   ▨ Nenets
□ Chukchi   ■ Saami

The Inuit ▶

The Inuit are the most widespread group in the Arctic. Thousands of years ago, they settled the Arctic coasts of North America and Greenland and lived by hunting land and sea creatures, including seals, fish and whales. Until modern times (see page 19), the Inuit spent their life migrating between summer and winter camps, carrying possessions on sledges pulled by husky dogs. They sailed Arctic waters in canoes called kayaks and in larger boats called umiaks.

An Inuit family repair a wooden sledge.

Husky

◀ Arctic homes

Traditionally, Arctic peoples used local materials to build shelters. The Inuit lived in turf and stone hu[t] with whalebone rafters. Some built domed iglo[o] with blocks of snow. Siberian peoples lived in tepee-style tents covered with reindeer hide.

Reindeer herders

Although few do so now, the Saami (below) and peoples of Siberia traditionally lived as nomadic reindeer herders. They followed the reindeer on their long migrations, moving south for winter and north again in spring. Reindeer provide meat, milk and hides for clothing and shelter. Bones and antlers were traditionally used to make weapons and tools.

An Arctic hunter kills a reindeer. Nothing will be wasted.

Arctic explorers ▶

The Vikings were the first Europeans to visit the Arctic. During the 10th century, they established colonies in Greenland and Iceland. From the 16th century, European sailors visited Arctic waters in an effort to find new sea routes from Europe to China and the East via northern Canada or Siberia. The seas proved too icy for shipping, and many expeditions failed.

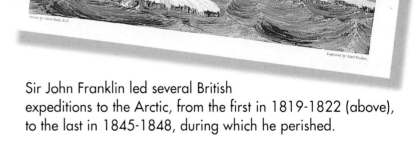

Sir John Franklin led several British expeditions to the Arctic, from the first in 1819-1822 (above), to the last in 1845-1848, during which he perished.

European explorers visited the polar regions from the 16th century onwards.

Q: Who were the first to reach the North and South Poles?

A: From the 1890s onwards, European explorers raced one another to be first to the Poles. In 1909, American explorer Robert Peary reached the North Pole with the help of Inuit husky teams. In 1911, Norwegian explorer Roald Amundsen was first to the South Pole.

CHAPTER THREE

Damaging the Polar Regions

Polar harvest

The polar regions are rich in resources, including living creatures. Following in the footsteps of the early Viking explorers, Europeans began to visit these frozen places to harvest the abundance of the seas. Whale-hunting began in the Arctic in the 1600s, and boomed until the 1800s. Whaling was a hard and dangerous life.

Whale-hunting ▼

Early whalers attacked the whales from small boats with hand-held harpoons. In the late 19th century, the invention of harpoon guns made the killing easier.

Fresh hunting grounds

By the late 1800s, so many whales had been killed that they became scarce in the Arctic. Most were killed by European and American whalers, but the Inuit (right) and other northern peoples also hunted whales for food. Meanwhile, in the 1820s, sealers sighted land in the Southern Ocean, which led to the discovery of Antarctica. Explorers reported seeing many whales in Antarctic waters and from the early 1900s, these too were hunted to near-extinction.

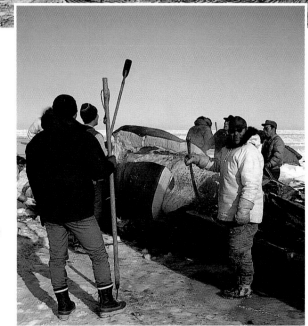

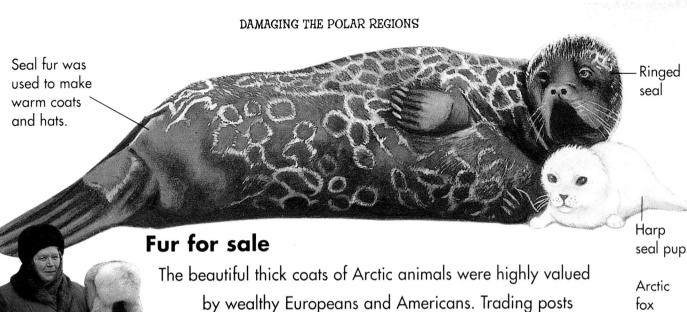

Seal fur was used to make warm coats and hats.

Ringed seal

Harp seal pup

Arctic fox

Fur for sale

The beautiful thick coats of Arctic animals were highly valued by wealthy Europeans and Americans. Trading posts were set up across the Arctic. The animals were usually caught by Arctic peoples, who then exchanged them at the trading posts for guns, alcohol, blankets and clothing.

▼ Changing lives

Few modern Arctic people live in the ways their ancestors did. Instead of hunting and herding, most earn their living through paid work, either in the Arctic or in cities down south. Arctic hunters use modern rifles instead of harpoons, and travel by plane instead of sledge and kayak.

Many Arctic people now travel by snow scooter.

TALKING POINT Between 1600 and the mid-1900s, Europeans slaughtered many thousands of polar whales.

Q: What did they use the whales for?

A: European whalers boiled whale blubber to make oil. Back home, the oil was used to light lamps, and make soap and margarine. Bony baleen from the whale's mouth was used to make corsets, umbrellas and other objects.

Mining and development

Some areas of the Arctic have rich mineral deposits. All land in the Arctic now forms part of Scandinavia, Russia, Canada or the USA. Around 1900, gold was discovered in northern Canada and Alaska. Important oil and gas fields have since been discovered and, most recently, diamonds have been found in northern Canada

▲ Antarctic minerals

No one knows exactly what minerals exist in Antarctica since 99% of this continent is buried under deep ice. It is likely that there are valuable minerals, but to protect the environment, no mining is now allowed there. Based on areas which their explorers were first to discover, several countries claim territory in Antarctica, in certain cases claiming the same land. In 1959, these countries signed the Antarctic Treaty, agreeing to suspend their territorial claims and work together.

▲ Gold-diggers

Around 1900, gold was discovered on the Klondike in Canada's Yukon Territory and at several places in Alaska. A gold rush started, as thousands of prospectors flooded north in the hope of striking it rich. New towns such as Dawson City sprang up to house the settlers. Similar development took place in Siberia, where gold was discovered at about the same time

◄ Mining in the Arctic

The Arctic holds rich stocks of silver, uranium, tin, diamonds, iron, lead, zinc and coal, as well as gold. Although the arrival of mining companies brought jobs and wealth to some regions, Arctic peoples who had lived on the land for centuries were forced to move. The mines themselves, although profitable, damage the environment by scarring the countryside and causing pollution.

Oil and gas ▶

In 1968, huge deposits of oil and natural gas were discovered on the seabed off Prudhoe Bay in Alaska. The oil companies quickly moved in, bringing further development to the region. Now 6,000 people live and work at Prudhoe Bay.

◀ Pipe down!

Transporting oil from Prudhoe Bay by ship was difficult because the seas were often frozen. In 1974-77, the Trans-Alaska Pipeline was built to carry the oil south to the ice-free port of Valdez. The pipeline is raised up off the ground to prevent damage to the permafrost.

◀ Transport links

Roads and railways were also built across the Arctic to ferry minerals south. These can damage the fragile tundra vegetation, which takes many years to recover. Roads and rail tracks also cause problems where they cut across reindeer migration routes.

TALKING POINT

The 1959 Antarctic Treaty resolved land claims in Antarctica.

Q: Who now owns the Antarctic continent?

A: No one "owns" Antarctica. By 1950, the overlapping land claims made by seven nations seemed likely to lead to war. In signing the 1959 treaty, these nations gave up their claims and agreed that Antarctica could only be used for peaceful purposes such as scientific research.

Pollution

Some human activities in the Arctic, such as mining, cause pollution. In 1989, the supertanker *Exxon Valdez*, carrying oil out from Alaska, hit a rock and spilled its cargo into the sea. The natural world is also damaged by pollution created elsewhere and carried to the polar regions by winds and ocean currents.

▲ Oil spill

Oil from the wrecked *Exxon Valdez* tanker polluted 1,900 km of coastline in Alaska. Although some marine birds and mammals were rescued, many thousands died when their fur or feathers became clogged with oil. The clean-up operation cost huge sums of money.

Ozone hole

Ozone loss in the atmosphere over the polar regions has caused another environmental problem. Ozone is a gas that screens out harmful ultraviolet (UV) light from the Sun. UV light can cause health problems such as skin cancers. Ozone loss is caused by chemicals called CFCs, found in fridges and spray cans.

This satellite image shows the ozone hole over Antarctica in white. The hole now appears every spring.

A thinning ozone layer means we need to take more care to protect ourselves from the Sun's harmful UV rays.

◄ Nuclear pollution

In 1986, a distant disaster caused pollution in the Arctic. A nuclear reactor at Chernobyl in the Ukraine caught fire and released a cloud of radioactive gas. The cloud drifted north and fell as rain over the Arctic tundra and nearby forests. Plants became polluted, and contaminated the reindeer that ate them. Thousands of animals had to be destroyed.

Greenhouse effect

"Greenhouse gases" in the atmosphere trap the Sun's heat and warm our planet. This natural process is called the greenhouse effect. But now, too many greenhouse gases in the atmosphere are trapping too much heat. This is raising temperatures worldwide.

Greenhouse gases

Some heat is trapped in the Earth's atmosphere.

Q: What difference would it make if the icecaps melted?

Global warming

World temperatures have risen by about 0.5°C over 100 years. Polar temperatures have risen faster – by about 2.5°C in Antarctica. The main greenhouse gas that causes global warming is carbon dioxide. It is produced as fossil fuels (coal, oil and gas) are burned in homes, cars, factories and power stations.

A: If all the ice in the polar regions melted, sea levels around the world would rise, causing widespread flooding. Low-lying countries such as Bangladesh and Holland would be largely underwater. If temperatures rise and warm the world's oceans, the seawater will expand, causing further flooding. However, scientists believe that global warming may also cause certain warm ocean currents to stop flowing. This would keep seawater cooler, which means it would not expand, and there would be less flooding.

Melting ice

There are signs that polar ice is melting as temperatures increase. In the late 1990s, a huge section of the Larsen Ice Shelf in Antarctica broke off and floated away. Scientists fear that the West Antarctic ice sheet might slide into the sea as other ice shelves break off. In the Arctic Ocean, measurements have shown that the sea ice, too, is thinning.

CHAPTER FOUR

Saving the Polar Regions

Controlling pollution

We now understand much more about what causes pollution and how it spreads to distant places like the polar regions. Scientists keep a careful watch on pollution levels in polar air, ice and water. The Antarctic is particularly important for scientific study because there are no mines or factories there to cause local pollution.

◀ Research on Antarctica

Since the Antarctic Treaty was signed in 1959, Antarctica has become a major centre for science. The continent now has over 80 research bases, run by many countries. Scientists study the rocks, ice, weather and marine life. In 1985, British Antarctic scientists made a major breakthrough when they discovered the hole in the ozone layer.

Marine pollution ▼

Scientists have discovered that the Arctic and Southern Oceans are polluted by poisonous waste dumped in far-away seas. Ocean currents carry the waste to polar seas, where it enters the food chain. Top predators such as polar bears are badly affected, because they eat many smaller creatures that absorb the pollution.

The dumped waste is mainly chemicals from industry and farming.

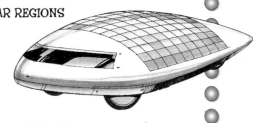

Clean energy

Scientists are working to develop "clean" energy sources, which generate power while causing less pollution. Electricity can be produced by harnessing the energy of winds, waves and sunlight, and cars (above) can be designed to run on solar power. Hydroelectricity, using flowing water, is a "clean" form of energy, but also causes problems as land is flooded to build the huge dams.

Wave "ducks" produce power from the waves.

Hydroelectric dams produce a lot of energy from falling water.

▼ Tackling pollution

In the 1990s, several international conferences were held to try to agree on action to reduce global warming and other pollution problems. Many nations agreed to limit their output of carbon dioxide, the main greenhouse gas. They also agreed to restrict the dumping of waste at sea, and stop producing CFCs, which scientists believe has already helped to save the ozone layer.

Representatives from different nations vote to curb pollution.

Q: Climate scientists are at work in the polar regions. Exactly how do they measure air pollution there?

A: The polar ice itself provides a record of pollution, both now and in the distant past. As ice builds up year after year, it records the air conditions that prevailed when the snow fell. Scientists drill deep into the ice to collect samples of ice that formed thousands of years ago. These help scientists to work out how much pollution has increased.

Protecting polar life

The polar regions are precious wild places where nature is still relatively untouched. They play a vital role in maintaining the world's climate balance, and also have great scientific value. We cannot allow damage to these unspoilt places to continue. In the last 30 years, many ordinary people have taken an interest in conservation – protecting the natural world.

Greenpeace protesters confront whalers in Antarctica.

Conservation

From the 1980s, protest groups such as Greenpeace campaigned against whaling, which had made whales scarce in the Antarctic. As a result, commercial whaling was banned in Antarctic waters. A similar campaign exposed cruelty in the sealing industry, where baby seals were killed for their fur. The protests were so successful that the seal fur trade collapsed.

Fighting overdevelopment ▶

From the 1970s, Arctic groups met to organise their response to development plans in their homelands. They laid claim to lands where their ancestors had lived for centuries, and fought plans for new mines, pipelines and dams that would damage the natural world. In Norway in the 1980s, the building of the Alta Dam (right) caused much protest from local Saami people trying to protect their land.

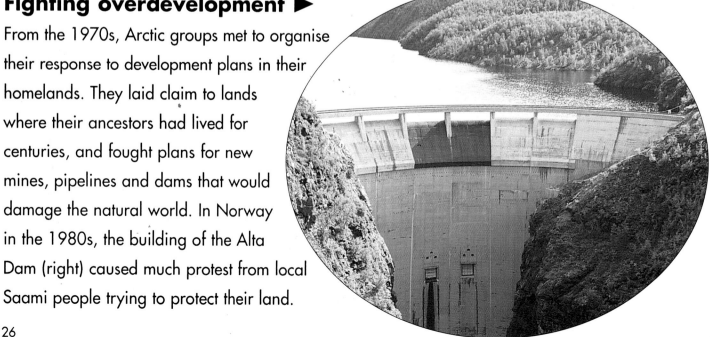

◄Welcome home!

In recent years, some Arctic groups have succeeded in winning back parts of their old homelands. In 1999, a large area in northern Canada was handed back to the Inuit. The region is the size of Norway. It is called Nunavut, an Inuit word which means "our land".

Arctic groups celebrate as Nunavut is handed over in 1999.

Animals like musk oxen, caribou and wolves are now in reserves and safe from hunting.

Wildlife sanctuaries

Large parts of the polar regions are now protected as wildlife sanctuaries. The whole of Antarctica and the surrounding ocean is now a protected area where no mining or drilling is allowed. The Arctic also has major reserves, including one of the world's largest in northern Greenland. Tourists visit the reserves to find out about wildlife.

TALKING POINT

Q: Now ordinary people as well as scientists can visit the Arctic and Antarctica. Is tourism big business in the polar regions?

A: It is growing, both in the Arctic and Antarctica. Most tourists visit in summer, which some say disturbs animals when they are breeding. But many visitors return home to join conservation groups. They join the fight to protect these wild, beautiful lands.

Look Back and Find

Now it's time to test your knowledge of the polar regions! Here are some questions about the topics covered in this book. The pictures will guide you to the right page if you need to check your answers.

Where in the world?

Where do the polar regions lie and why are they so cold? Why does the Earth experience seasons? The Arctic and Antarctic are known as the lands of the midnight sun. Can you think why? Why doesn't Antarctica appear on many world maps?

Frozen ocean

In what ways are the Arctic and Antarctic similar? How are they different? Which natural features are commonly found on the Arctic tundra? What name is given to permanently frozen ground that lies below the topsoil? What special danger for ships lurks in polar seas?

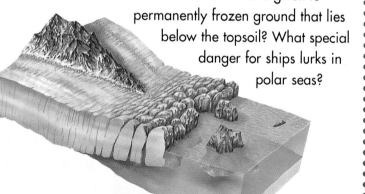

Icy land

Why is Antarctica the coldest place on Earth? Antarctic coasts are warmer than areas far inland. Why do you think this is? Was Antarctica always as cold as it is today? Scientists know quite a lot about Antarctica's distant past. How do they know?

Marine life

Name four different kinds of polar sea creature. What special features help them to survive in the icy seas? How does a marine food chain work? All life in the polar oceans depends on sunlight. Can you explain why? Why do many sea creatures migrate to the polar regions in spring?

Plants and animals on land

How many different creatures can you name that live in the Arctic? Compared with the Arctic, very few plants and animals are found in Antarctica. Why do you think this is? How do Arctic animals hide from their enemies? Some animals live in the Arctic all year round. How do they survive in winter?

Humans in the polar regions

Name three different groups of people who live in the Arctic. What was their main food traditionally? There is very little wood in the Arctic. Before modern times, how did Arctic people build shelters and make tools and weapons? Why did Europeans first visit the Arctic?

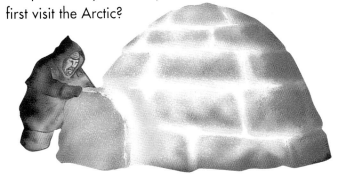

Polar life in danger

Sea creatures such as whales were the first resources to be exploited by Europeans in the Arctic. What did they do with the whales they killed? How did whale-hunting methods change over the years? What happened when whales became scarce in the Arctic? Who discovered Antarctica? Do Arctic peoples still live as their ancestors did?

Mineral riches

Why aren't minerals being mined in Antarctica? What precious metal found in the Arctic sent thousands of prospectors rushing north? In 1968, mining companies announced they had found "black gold" at Prudhoe Bay in Alaska. What do you think they meant? How are the minerals mined in the Arctic carried south?

Damaging the sea and air

What are some of the main causes of pollution in the polar regions? Can you name a bad accident that affected Arctic marine life? What chemicals are damaging the ozone layer in the atmosphere? What is the greenhouse effect and how does it work? Humans are responsible for global warming. How? Is global warming affecting the polar regions?

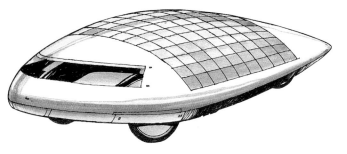

Solving pollution problems

Why is Antarctica important to the study of pollution? What global problem was first discovered there in 1985? How do marine predators become polluted by waste dumped at sea? What can we do about global warming? Why do scientists sample ice from deep below the surface to find out about pollution?

Saving polar life

What measures are being taken to protect life in the polar regions? Can ordinary people help with conservation? Do any traditional Arctic groups now hold land in the far north? Does large-scale whaling still go on in the Southern Ocean? Do you think tourism in the polar regions is a good or a bad thing?

You Be Environmental!

The polar regions may seem a very long way away, but we can all do things that help to save them. Everyone can help to reduce the pollution that causes global warming by saving energy both at home and at school. Manufacturing the packaging for the food we buy at supermarkets uses up a lot of energy. Later, most packaging is just thrown away. Return used glass, cans and paper to a recycling bank. It all helps to save energy!

Used bottles, cans, clothes and newspapers can all be recycled.

Useful addresses

World Wide Fund for Nature
Panda House, Weyside Park,
Catteshall Lane, Godalming,
Surrey GU7 1XR
website: www.wwf-uk.org

Greenpeace
Canonbury Villas,
London N1 2PN
website: www.greenpeace.co.uk

Friends of the Earth
26-28 Underwood Street,
London N1 7JQ
website:
www.foe.co.uk

◄ **Make a poster**

Make a poster about the polar regions and saving energy to help spread the word at your school. The poster could point out that recycling and switching off unwanted lights and heaters saves energy. Riding a bike, walking or using public transport also saves energy and causes less pollution than using private cars. You could also write to your MP to keep up the pressure on the government to curb output of greenhouse gases.

GLOSSARY

Axis
An imaginary line running through the centre of the Earth between the North and South Poles.

Blubber
A layer of fat found under the skin of whales, seals and polar bears, which keeps them warm.

Caribou
The wild reindeer of North America.

CFCs
Stands for chlorofluorocarbons – chemicals used in the manufacture of spray cans and refrigerators, which harm the ozone layer.

Conservation
The protection of the natural world.

Fossil fuels
Fossilised remains of ancient plants that have been changed to form deposits of coal, oil or natural gas.

Glacier
A mass of frozen ice which flows slowly downhill towards the coast.

Global warming
A rise in temperatures worldwide, caused by the build-up of carbon dioxide and other "greenhouse gases" in the atmosphere.

Greenhouse effect
The warming of the Earth's atmosphere caused by certain gases which trap heat from the Sun near the planet's surface.

Hydroelectric power
Electricity generated from running water.

Iceberg
A large block of floating ice that has broken off from a glacier at the coast. Six-sevenths of an iceberg's bulk lies below the water surface.

Icecap
A mass of ice which permanently covers most land in the polar regions.

Ice shelf
A vast slab of floating ice joined to the land.

Igloo
The Inuit word for a dome-shaped shelter built from ice blocks.

Krill
Small, shrimp-like sea creatures.

Ozone layer
A natural form of oxygen which forms a layer in the Earth's atmosphere and protects the Earth from harmful ultraviolet radiation in sunlight.

Permafrost
The permanently frozen ground that lies beneath the topsoil in the polar regions.

Plankton
Tiny marine plants and animals that form the base of the food chain in polar seas.

Taiga
A belt of forested land found south of the Arctic tundra.

Tundra
The barren, treeless plains of the far north.

INDEX

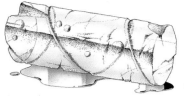

Picture credits

Abbreviations: t-top, m-middle, b-bottom, r-right, l-left, c-centre

Cover t, 4, 6, 7, 13 both, 20tl, 26ml - Digital Stock. Cover c, 3tl, 23b - G. Richards. 5m, 24tr - Anne Hawthorne/B&C Alexander. 5, 18br, 19tl, 21tr, 21ml - Steve McCutcheon/FLPA. 8, 22ml - Mark Newman/FLPA. 9ml - Christina Carvalho/FLPA. 9mr - Winifred Wisniewski. 10, 24ml - E&D Hosking/FLPA. 11- NASA/Oxford Scientific Films. 12 - Jeff Foott/BBC Natural History Unit. 14 - Robert Pickett/CORBIS. 15, 17 both, 27 both - B&C Alexander. 18m - Frank Lane/FLPA. 20m - Museum of History & Industry/CORBIS. 20bl - Julian Dowdeswell/B&C Alexander. 22bl - Caroline Penn/CORBIS. 23ml - Roger Tidman. 26br - Knudsens Fotosenter.

Christian art and writing

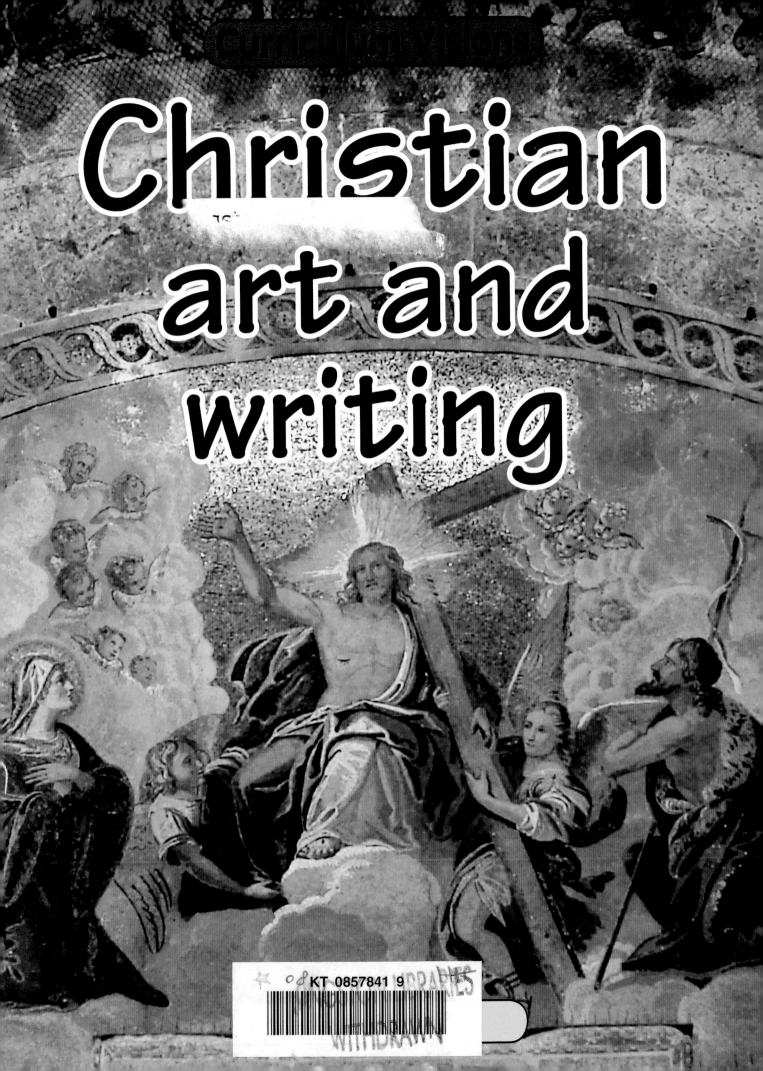

Glossary

ADVENT The word advent means coming, or arrival, and in Christianity, Advent is the time of year that includes the four Sundays before Christmas.

APOSTLES The first followers of Jesus. They were given a special job by Jesus – to carry on his teachings after he died.

CRUCIFIXION The ancient Romans often killed criminals and others by nailing them to a large cross. This is the way Jesus was killed, and when Christians use the word crucifixion they are talking about the death of Christ.

EASTER The Christian holy day, or feast day that celebrates the resurrection of Christ. It is celebrated on the Sunday following the first full moon after the vernal equinox.

EPIPHANY A holy day, or feast day, that is the twelfth day of Christmas. This is the day that the three kings visited the baby Jesus in the manger and brought him gifts. Epiphany falls on 6 January.

GOOD FRIDAY A holy day that takes place on the Friday before Easter. This is the day when Jesus was crucified and died on the cross.

HOLY SPIRIT The Holy Spirit is the part of God that people can see on Earth. In other words, when God wants to do something on Earth that people can see, the action is said to be done by the Holy Spirit.

LENT This is a period of 40 days before Easter. It is a time when Christians prepare for Easter by giving up something that is important to them, such as eating meat.

NATIVITY This word means birth, and in Christianity the nativity means the birth of Jesus.

ORTHODOX A type of Christianity that is practised in Russia, Greece, Ethiopia and a few other places.

PENTECOST This holiday takes place 50 days after the Jewish holy day of Passover. The original apostles (who were Jewish) gathered on this day to celebrate, and the Holy Spirit came to them in the form of flames. After this, the apostles preached Jesus' teachings.

RESURRECTION Rebirth. After his death, Jesus was resurrected – he came back to Earth to show his followers that he was with God.

ROMAN CATHOLIC A Christian who follows the Pope of Rome as the leader of the Catholic Church. Roman Catholic priests cannot marry and Roman Catholics have some special ceremonies that they observe.

SEASON In Christianity, a time of year when a particular holy day or holy time is observed, for example, the Christmas season, or the Lenten season.

STATIONS OF THE CROSS These are the places where certain things happened to Jesus while he was on his way to be crucified. Also, plaques in churches that are reminders of these events.

SYMBOL An object, image, picture or letter that has a special meaning. Some symbols can have more than one meaning.